LEE EVANS ARRANGES JEROME KERN

Revised Edition

ISBN 978-1-4234-0803-1

HAL•LEONARD® CORPORATION

7777 W. BLUEMOUND RD. P.O. BOX 13819 MILWAUKEE, WI 53213

T0057638

Visit Hal Leonard Online at
www.halleonard.com

FOREWORD

In order to give the reader a better sense of the
creative development and genius of Jerome Kern,
the songs in this volume appear in the
order of copyright date.

Lee Evans

LOOK FOR THE SILVER LINING

from SALLY

Words by BUDDY DeSYLVA
Music by JEROME KERN

4

THEY DIDN'T BELIEVE ME

from THE GIRL FROM UTAH

Words by HERBERT REYNOLDS
Music by JEROME KERN

Ballad style; rubato; with warm expression

SUNNY
from SUNNY

Lyrics by OSCAR HAMMERSTEIN II and OTTO HARBACH
Music by JEROME KERN

14

WHO?
from SUNNY

Lyrics by OTTO HARBACH
and OSCAR HAMMERSTEIN II
Music by JEROME KERN

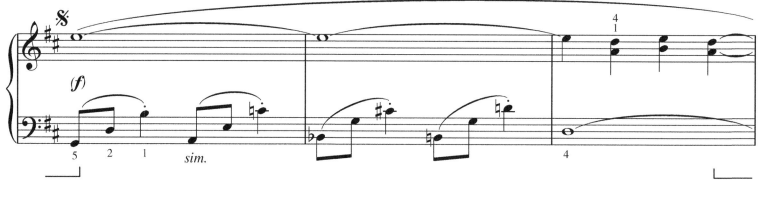

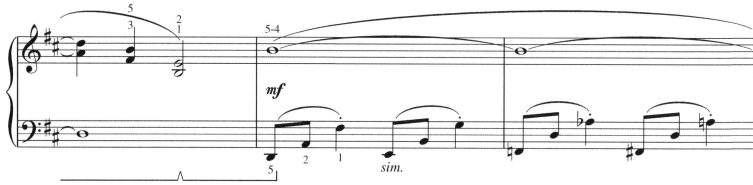

WHY WAS I BORN?
from SWEET ADELINE

Lyrics by OSCAR HAMMERSTEIN II
Music by JEROME KERN

WHY DO I LOVE YOU?
from SHOW BOAT

Lyrics by OSCAR HAMMERSTEIN II
Music by JEROME KERN

Ballad style; with movement
Chorus

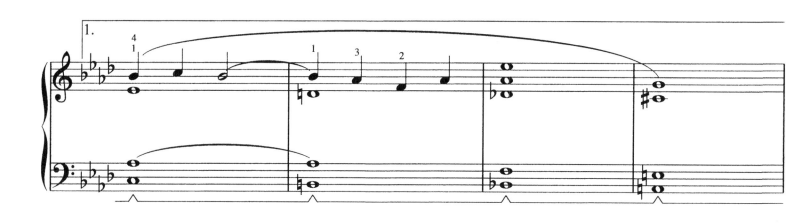

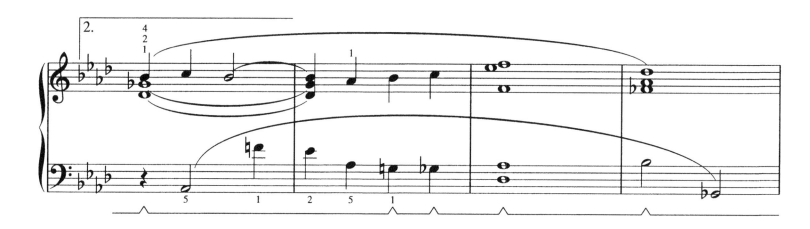

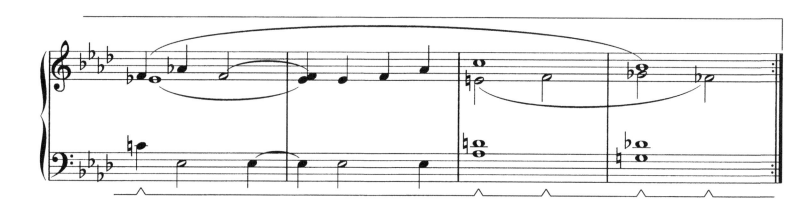

BILL
from SHOW BOAT

Music by JEROME KERN
Words by P.G. WODEHOUSE
and OSCAR HAMMERSTEIN II

MAKE BELIEVE
from SHOW BOAT

Lyrics by OSCAR HAMMERSTEIN II
Music by JEROME KERN

OL' MAN RIVER
from SHOW BOAT

Lyrics by OSCAR HAMMERSTEIN II
Music by JEROME KERN

With movement and flow; not too slowly; rubato
VERSE

Slowly, with deep expression
CHORUS

CAN'T HELP LOVIN' DAT MAN
from SHOW BOAT

Lyrics by OSCAR HAMMERSTEIN II
Music by JEROME KERN

CHORUS

YOU ARE LOVE
from SHOW BOAT

Lyrics by OSCAR HAMMERSTEIN II
Music by JEROME KERN

THE SONG IS YOU
from MUSIC IN THE AIR

Lyrics by OSCAR HAMMERSTEIN II
Music by JEROME KERN

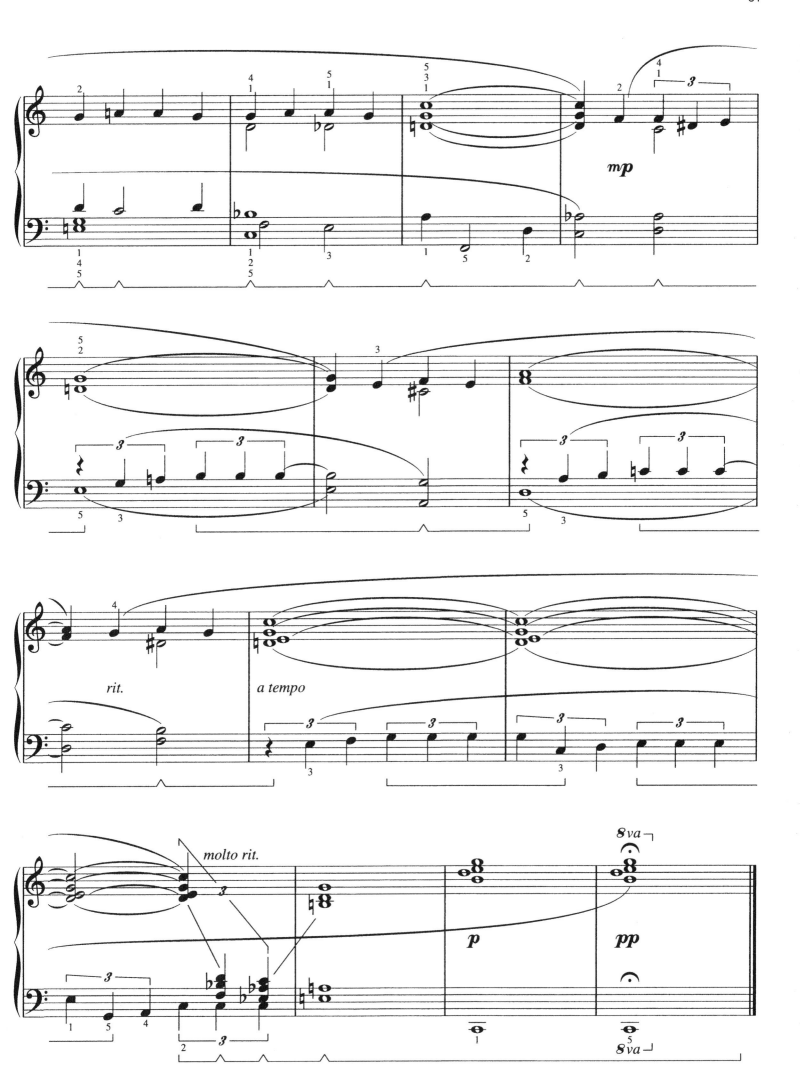

I'VE TOLD EV'RY LITTLE STAR

from MUSIC IN THE AIR

Lyrics by OSCAR HAMMERSTEIN II
Music by JEROME KERN

Chorus

YESTERDAYS
from ROBERTA

Words by OTTO HARBACH
Music by JEROME KERN

SMOKE GETS IN YOUR EYES
from ROBERTA

Words by OTTO HARBACH
Music by JEROME KERN

I WON'T DANCE
from ROBERTA

Words and Music by JIMMY McHUGH,
DOROTHY FIELDS, JEROME KERN,
OSCAR HAMMERSTEIN II and OTTO HARBACH

Brightly (♩ = 116) (♫ and ♩. ♪ played as ⌐³⌐ ♩ ♪)

a tempo   R.H.

Chorus

1.

LOVELY TO LOOK AT

from ROBERTA

Words and Music by JIMMY McHUGH,
DOROTHY FIELDS and JEROME KERN

I DREAM TOO MUCH

Words and Music by DOROTHY FIELDS
and JEROME KERN

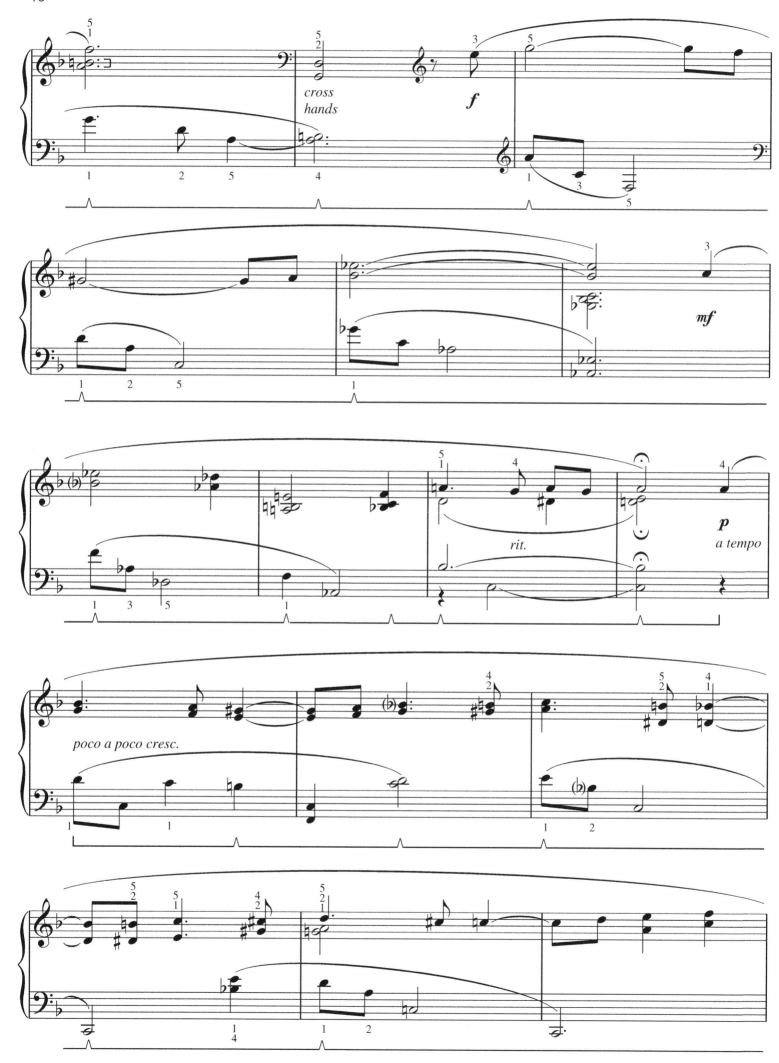

WALTZ IN SWINGTIME

Words and Music by DOROTHY FIELDS
and JEROME KERN

Tempo di Valse; brightly   (Straight 8ths)

84

PICK YOURSELF UP
from SWING TIME

Words by DOROTHY FIELDS
Music by JEROME KERN

A FINE ROMANCE

from SWING TIME

Words by DOROTHY FIELDS
Music by JEROME KERN

THE WAY YOU LOOK TONIGHT
from SWING TIME

Words by DOROTHY FIELDS
Music by JEROME KERN

Warmly, but with motion; ballad style

D.S. al Coda

CODA

molto rit.

a tempo

8va

THE FOLKS WHO LIVE ON THE HILL

from HIGH, WIDE AND HANDSOME

Lyrics by OSCAR HAMMERSTEIN II
Music by JEROME KERN

ALL THE THINGS YOU ARE

from VERY WARM FOR MAY

Lyrics by OSCAR HAMMERSTEIN II
Music by JEROME KERN

103

With expression
CHORUS

a tempo

THE LAST TIME I SAW PARIS

from LADY, BE GOOD

Lyrics by OSCAR HAMMERSTEIN II
Music by JEROME KERN

Chorus
Simply; with a sense of flow

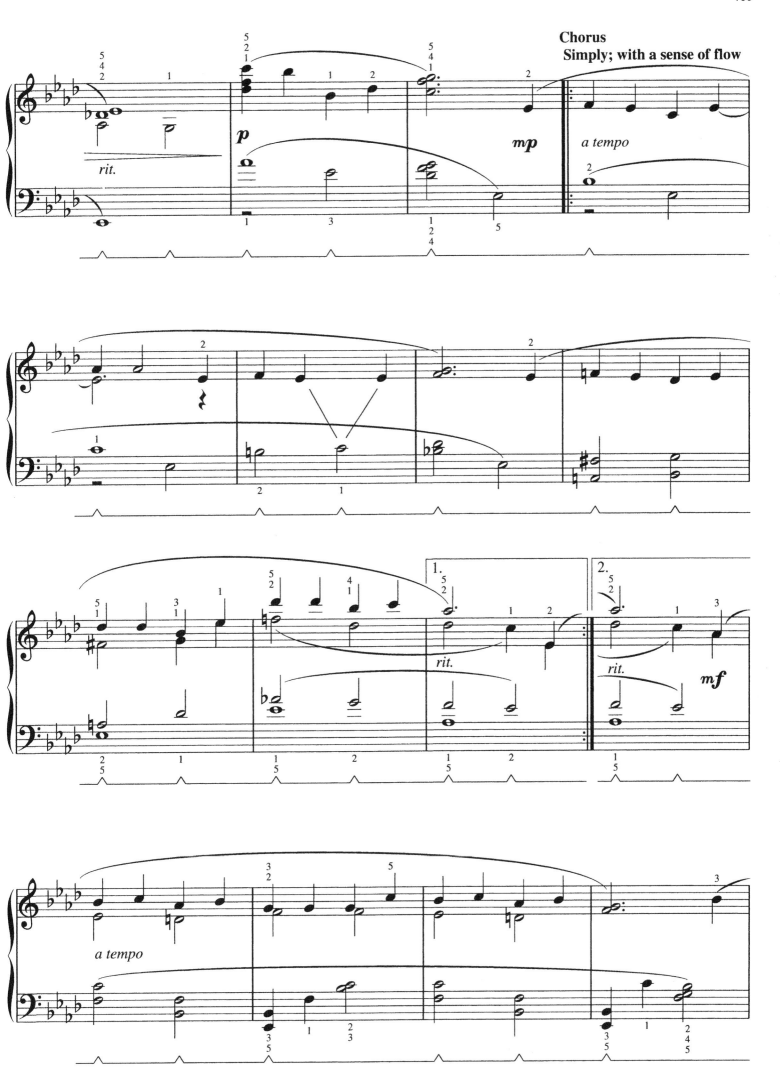

I'M OLD FASHIONED

from YOU WERE NEVER LOVELIER

Words by JOHNNY MERCER
Music by JEROME KERN

DEARLY BELOVED
from YOU WERE NEVER LOVELIER

Music by JEROME KERN
Words by JOHNNY MERCER

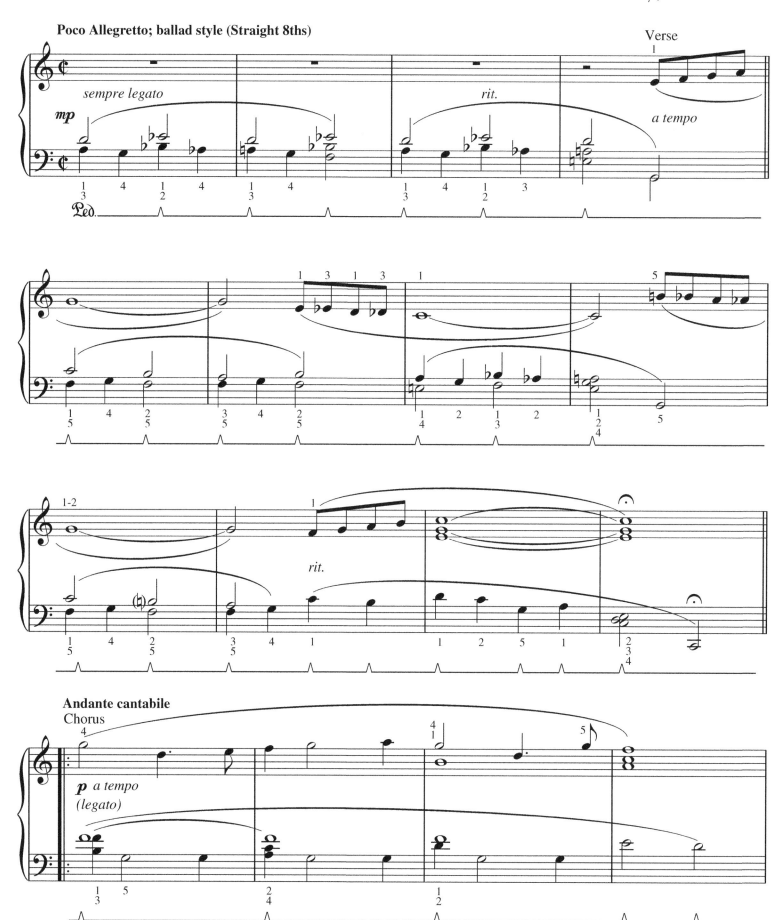

LONG AGO (AND FAR AWAY)

from COVER GIRL

Words by IRA GERSHWIN
Music by JEROME KERN

Moderate ballad; with motion; rubato (circa ♩ = 66)